Essential Question
What are different kinds of energy?

W9-AXT-142

The Fuel of the Future

by Vanessa York

Introduction

Fuel is any material that stores energy that can be **extracted** and then used. We use fuel to run vehicles and machines. We also use fuel to make electricity.

We need fuel to help us get around.

diesel fumes

truck

Diesel fumes from trucks cause pollution.

Fossil fuels are fuels such as coal, natural gas, and oil. We find these fuels in the ground. There are some big problems with fossil fuels. Fossil fuels cause pollution. Fossil fuels also produce greenhouse gases. Greenhouse gases may cause global warming. We are also running out of fossil fuels. Many people think finding other kinds of fuels is a smart thing to do.

In Other Words becoming harder to find. En español, *running out of* quiere decir *acabándose*.

CHAPTER 1

Biofuels

Biofuel is a renewable fuel. Biofuel is made from plants such as soy beans. Biofuel is also made from natural waste products such as animal fat and used vegetable oil. Biofuel produces less pollution than traditional fuels.

Plant Sugars and Ethanol

Plants are full of sugar. The sugar can be extracted to make a biofuel called ethanol. Ethanol can be used in cars.

David Nunuk/Science Source

Corn is processed at this bioethanol plant in Iowa.

Henry Ford's Model T was first designed to run on ethanol.

hat

windshield

Biofuel is not a new idea. Rudolf Diesel invented the diesel engine. Diesel knew gasoline was not easily available at that time. In 1900, Diesel showed his engine running on peanut oil. Henry Ford expected his Model T car to run on ethanol produced from corn. Today, people are trying to use biofuels again.

Some buses use biofuel.

Oramstock/Alamy Stock Photo

The most common type of biofuel used is bioethanol. Bioethanol is made from plants such as wheat, potatoes, corn, and sugar beets. Bioethanol can also be made from seaweed.

Ethanol is mostly used to run cars. In Brazil, about one out of every two cars runs on ethanol.

Ethanol Fuel Production in 2015

United States	14,800 million gallons
Brazil	7,093 million gallons
European Union	1,387 million gallons
China	813 million gallons
Canada	436 million gallons

Source: www.afdc.energy.gov

Biofuel, such as bioethanol, does not pollute the environment as much as gasoline does. However, it can still harm the environment. It takes seven acres of corn to produce enough bioethanol to run one car for one year. That's a lot of land that could also be used to produce food. In some places, forests have been cut down to make room for biofuel crops.

corn

Corn is grown for biofuel, as well as for food.

Grown for Biofuel

Dave Reede/All Canada Photos/Getty Images

7

scientist

plants

This scientist is researching plant bacteria that may be useful in making biofuel.

Biobutanol is made from plants. Scientists are excited by this biofuel. <u>They've</u> found that biobutanol can be made by bacteria such as *E. coli.* *E. coli* can cause an upset stomach!

Biobutanol costs a lot to produce. But if scientists keep studying this fuel, they may improve the way they make biobutanol. That would make it a renewable fuel that could replace fossil fuels.

Language Detective   They've is a pronoun-verb contraction. What two words make up *they've*?

Lawrence Berkeley National Laboratory/Photo Researchers, Inc.

Biodiesel is made from oils or fats, such as soybean and palm oil. Scientists have even made biodiesel from coffee grounds!

Biodiesel looks like ordinary diesel. Diesel is a fuel made from oil. Ordinary diesel is harmful to Earth. Biodiesel is better than diesel because it is **nontoxic** and **biodegradable**.

Diesel Is used to run heavy machinery as well as many cars and trucks.

digger

truck

Some people can buy biodiesel at their gas stations. Biodiesel causes less pollution than ordinary diesel, but biodiesel still produces pollution. Biodiesel costs a lot to make. Scientists are looking at ways to improve this fuel. But maybe there are other clean fuels out there.

Earthrace
Around the World

The powerboat *Earthrace* ran on biodiesel. In 2008, *Earthrace* broke the world speed record for going around the world.

Bil Philpot/Alamy Stock Photo

STOP AND CHECK

What are some of the problems with biofuels?

CHAPTER 2

Hydrogen Fuel

In the future, all cars may run on water. Hydrogen is a gas with no color and no smell. Hydrogen can be burned as a fuel. It produces almost no pollution.

rocket

Stocktrek/age fotostock

Hydrogen is found in water. Hydrogen is also found in **hydrocarbons**. Hydrocarbons are in many fuels, such as gasoline and natural gas.

NASA uses hydrogen fuel to launch rockets.

Making hydrogen fuel takes a lot of energy. It also costs a lot of money. If scientists keep researching hydrogen fuel, it will be easier to make.

Today, hydrogen fuel is mostly used in fuel cells. Fuel cells combine, or bring together, hydrogen and oxygen. This causes a chemical reaction. Fuel cells produce electricity.

Hydrogen Power

Italy has a hydrogen power plant giving power to 20,000 homes. It prevents thousands of tons of greenhouse gases each year.

Hydrogen power helps provide electricity to the city of Venice, Italy.

Hydrogen fuel may be a fuel of the future. Biofuels cause pollution, but hydrogen fuel does not. In fact, some cars and airplanes already run on hydrogen fuel.

STOP AND CHECK

What is one benefit of hydrogen as a fuel? What is one problem with it?

A Hydrogen Fuel Cell

Hydrogen fuel cells produce electricity and water. This water is so clean that astronauts in space drink it!

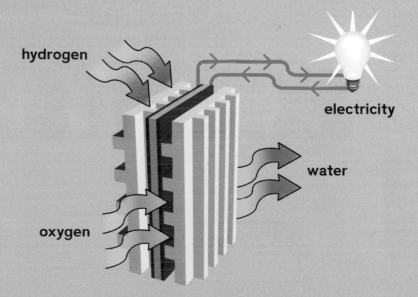

hydrogen

electricity

water

oxygen

Conclusion

The fuels of the future must be renewable, or always available. Scientists are looking for new ways to do things. Their work will make fuels cost less to produce.

We must make good use of Earth's resources. Not all of Earth's resources are renewable.

This racing car is powered by hydrogen fuel.

Car Culture, Inc./Car Culture® Collection/Getty Images

Summarize

Use details from *The Fuel of the Future* to summarize the text. Your graphic organizer may help you.

Cause	→	Effect
First	→	
Next	→	
Then	→	
Finally	→	

Text Evidence

1. *The Fuel of the Future* is an argumentative text. Argumentative texts give facts and examples to make the reader agree with the author's opinion. Find two pieces of information the author uses to persuade the reader. GENRE

2. How does using fossil fuels affect the environment? CAUSE AND EFFECT

3. Homophones are words that sound the same but have different meanings. Find the homophones on page 5. HOMOPHONES

4. Write a paragraph about the effects hydrogen would have if it became a popular fuel. WRITE ABOUT READING

Compare Texts
Read about ways you and your family can save energy.

Saving Energy

Using more energy uses more resources. Using less energy helps the planet. It saves money, too.

There are many simple ways we can save energy. Often these ways are just common sense. All you need to do is think about it.

Keeping doors, curtains, and blinds closed when it is cold saves energy. Keeping doors and windows open when it is hot cools the air without using energy.

In Other Words   reasonable ideas. En español, *common sense* quiere decir *ideas razonables*.

Wasting water also wastes energy. It takes a lot of electricity to supply water and take away dirty water.

Wasting electricity also wastes energy. Turn off the lights if you are leaving a room. Use energy-saving lightbulbs. Turn off televisions. Computers should be turned off when you aren't using them.

If you leave a room, switch off the light behind you.

TOP TIPS TO SAVE ENERGY

1. **Turn it off!** If you're finished with the lights, the television, or the stereo, turn it off.

2. **Keep it closed!** The refrigerator and the oven both work better when their doors are closed. Closing doors inside the house keeps heat in.

3. **Look for the label!**
Washing machines, refrigerators, and dryers that use less energy have a special "energy star" label. You can also get lightbulbs that save energy.

lightbulb →

Mike Kemp/Rubberball/Getty Images

An energy-efficient lightbulb uses little electricity.

Make Connections
What do you think was the main idea in *Saving Energy*? ESSENTIAL QUESTION

What theme does *The Fuel of the Future* share with *Saving Energy*? TEXT TO TEXT

Glossary

biodegradable able to decompose, or break down, naturally *(page 9)*

extracted taken out of something or from somewhere *(page 2)*

fossil fuels fuels, such as coal, that are found in the ground *(page 3)*

global warming the increase in Earth's surface temperature due to the greenhouse effect *(page 3)*

greenhouse gases gases, such as carbon dioxide, that get trapped in Earth's atmosphere, which makes the atmosphere hotter *(page 3)*

hydrocarbons organic compounds of hydrogen and carbon, found in crude oil *(page 11)*

nontoxic safe or harmless to the environment *(page 9)*

Index

Focus on Science

Purpose To find out how a gas (carbon dioxide) rises from liquid

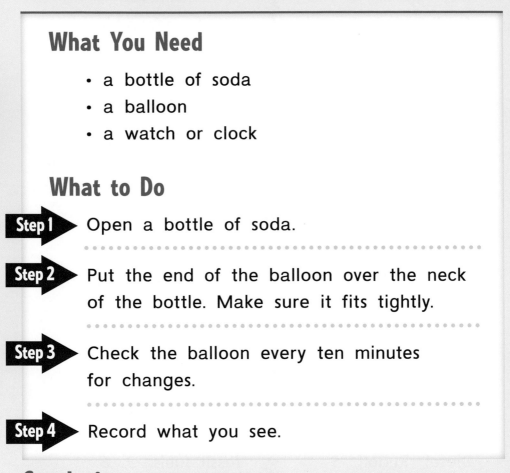

What You Need

- a bottle of soda
- a balloon
- a watch or clock

What to Do

Step 1 Open a bottle of soda.

Step 2 Put the end of the balloon over the neck of the bottle. Make sure it fits tightly.

Step 3 Check the balloon every ten minutes for changes.

Step 4 Record what you see.

Conclusion What happened to the balloon?